Original title:
Beneath the Tropical Sun

Copyright © 2025 Creative Arts Management OÜ
All rights reserved.

Author: Victor Mercer
ISBN HARDBACK: 978-1-80581-654-6
ISBN PAPERBACK: 978-1-80581-181-7
ISBN EBOOK: 978-1-80581-654-6

The Laughter of Ocean Waves

Waves giggle and splash, full of cheer,
The seagulls squawk jokes we all hear.
Shells laugh as they dance on the shore,
Who knew the ocean could be such a bore?

Sandcastles tumble, but we won't frown,
Each grain of sand is a comedian's crown.
Crabs tiptoe in, doing their dance,
In this beachy world, everyone has a chance.

Serenade of the Coconut Trees

Coconuts sway with their fuzzy heads,
Whispering tales that tickle our beds.
They giggle as monkeys swing by with flair,
Throwing down laughter, nuts everywhere!

Palm fronds wave like enthusiastic fans,
Cheering for beachgoers with quirky plans.
Each breeze carries a joke from the leaves,
Tropical giggles, what joy it weaves!

A Symphony in Sunset Colors

The sun dusk paints with a splash of fun,
As colors collide like kids on the run.
Pinks and oranges in a quirky blend,
Who knew the sky had such a playful trend?

Clouds puffy like cotton candy dreams,
Winking at surfers riding silly schemes.
Every hue chuckles, a radiant cheer,
As the sun dips down, day ends with a jeer.

Reflections on the Coral Reef

Fish flit and flash, playing hide and seek,
In the coral maze, it's a vibrant peak!
Laughter bubbles up from every hue,
The reef is alive with a comical crew.

Turtles wear glasses, pretending to read,
Crabs in tuxedos all take the lead.
Every coral whispers sweet little lies,
In this underwater world where humor flies.

The Call of the Monsoon Wind

The breeze arrives with a laugh,
Whipping hats from heads like a gaffe.
Puddles dance, splashes go wild,
Umbrellas flip—what a sight for a child!

Raindrops race with a cheeky spin,
Making roofs a bright, busy din.
Socks soaked through in a flash of glee,
Who knew rain could bring such jubilee?

Secrets of the Cascading Waterfall

Water tumbles down with a roar,
Fish slip past, "Not today!" they implore.
Splashing in foam like a person unseen,
Nature's soap opera in shades of green.

A frog leaps up, thinks he's a star,
Croaks out a tune, "Is it too bizarre?"
The rocks all smile, they know the show,
Round two begins, and off they go!

Journey Through the Foliage

Leaves rustle secrets, a playful tease,
Like whispers of friends in a summer breeze.
A monkey swings by, drops a coconut,
Laughs echo softly from inside its gut.

Vines tangle up in a dance of fun,
A game of twister 'neath the glowing sun.
Nature's party, with laughter afoot,
Who would've thought that mud could outglut?

Sweet Melodies of Island Nights

The twilight hums a magical song,
Crickets play tunes, but they're never wrong.
A firefly winks like a disco ball,
While the night sky paints a canvas for all.

Laughter erupts from a nearby stand,
As someone trips near the sandcastle band.
The ocean joins in, waves singing loud,
A night on the beach with joy unbowed!

Secrets in the Shade

Under leafy green, we play,
In the shade, we dance away.
Lemonade spills from my cup,
Giggles soon come bubbling up.

Sunglasses perched on my nose,
Silly hats with floppy bows.
While the lizards laugh and stare,
We plot mischief in the air.

Caught a crab, it's quite the feat,
Wiggling softly on my feet.
It escapes with a tiny pinch,
Calm as a breeze, I start to flinch.

We whisper secrets to the breeze,
Tell the coconuts our tease.
With every splash and silly song,
We make the day forever long.

Glistening Sands and Golden Dreams

On golden sands, we sculpt a throne,
A castle built from dreams, our own.
Seagulls swoop with critical eyes,
As we laugh at our lofty tries.

Footprints track our playful path,
In the sun, we feel its wrath.
I slip, I trip, into a wave,
Oh, the stories that we'll save!

Sandy snacks and sticky hands,
Finding treasures as the band stands.
Hammocks swinging like a tease,
We wonder, 'Can we catch the breeze?'

Each grain tells a story bright,
Of silly moments, pure delight.
As we bask in the sunlit beams,
We weave together golden dreams.

Echoes of the Palm Fronds

Palm fronds sway in cheeky dance,
We giggle at their leafy prance.
A monkey swings, a cheeky feat,
Stole my snack, oh what a treat!

The breeze whispers, so very low,
"Don't forget, it's time to go!"
But we're too busy splashing waves,
In our water forts, like brave knaves.

"Hey look, a crab!" I shout with glee,
But it scuttles off, oh woe is me.
The shells we gather, weird and strange,
Have me thinking 'bout a change.

We whisper tales to the day,
Of joys that dance and sweetly play.
And palm trees giggle in delight,
As we savor this silly night.

Hues of Paradise

Colors clash in the afternoon,
A rainbow's smile like a cartoon.
Flip-flops squeak as we parade,
Across the shore, our fun brigade.

With paint on cheeks, we look so bright,
A jellyfish caught in a bite.
Bubbles floating, chaos reigns,
As we laugh at all our stains.

The sunset's hues, a wild show,
We pretend to be the stars in tow.
The ocean whispers, 'Come and play,'
While our troubles drift away.

In this paradise of laughs and glows,
We journey where the cool wind blows.
With every giggle that we share,
We paint our world beyond compare.

Dappled Light in Green Canopies

In the jungle, monkeys swing,
Bananas fly—it's a wild fling.
Parrots squawk, a playful din,
Chasing lizards, ready to win.

Chameleons change their hue,
"Who wore it best?" they muse anew.
With sunburned backs, we laugh and sway,
Wishing lizards would just stay away.

Frogs in hats hop with flair,
Fashion shows under trees, oh so rare.
Sunshine dances on our skin,
As we trip over roots—we grin.

Dreaming of Distant Shores

A crab scuttles, sideways proud,
Dreaming of waves, oh, so loud.
With a tiny bucket and a spade,
He builds a castle, unafraid.

The seaweed wiggles, quite the show,
"I'm a mermaid!" shouts a toe.
As the tides come in, they sweep us all,
Sandcastles tumble, have a ball!

Seagulls squawk, plotting next meal,
While tourists sunbathe, start to squeal.
With sunscreen on noses, beach vibes bloom,
As beach balls bounce—and so does gloom.

A Tapestry of Tropical Colors

In a market filled with vibrant sights,
Papayas, pineapples, oh what delights.
A chef drops his knife—oh, what a blunder,
"Is it lunch or just a culinary thunder?"

Painted flowers in hats parade,
With dance moves that surely won't fade.
Bright hibiscus whispers naughty things,
While coconut drinks make laughter sing.

Kids throw coconuts, giggling with glee,
"Who's got the best arm?" We wait to see.
In this colorful world, let's not be shy,
With smiles that sparkle, let worries fly.

Silhouettes Against a Warm Canvas

As the sun sets, shadows grow,
Dancers sway with a cheeky flow.
Flamingos strut, so proud and bright,
As if they're stars, stealing the night.

A kid trips on a flip-flop lace,
Lands in the mud—oh, what a face!
With laughter echoing through the sand,
We all join in—life's quite unplanned!

Kites in the sky, colors that clash,
A wild breeze gives them a thrash.
As we watch the sunset's final bow,
We laugh at life—what a crazy wow!

Echoes of the Ocean's Heart

The dolphins dance, they love to play,
While seagulls squawk in a silly way.
The crabs do the cha-cha on the shore,
To the rhythm of waves, they beg for more.

A sunburnt tourist with a wild hat,
Tripped over a clam and said, "Well, that's that!"
The ocean's waves, they laugh and tease,
As sandy toes shake off the breeze.

A sea turtle dreaming of ice cream,
Swims through the surf like a googly beam.
With shells for friends, they giggle and glide,
In the salty world where fun won't hide.

Velvet Shadows on Golden Sands

The sun smiles wide, a brilliant grin,
While beach balls bounce like they're on a spin.
A seagull steals a chip from my snack,
And the sunburned kids all yell, "Get back!"

Picnic ants in a marching line,
Waving flags made of breadcrumbs, how divine!
The beach blanket's a pirate ship afloat,
Sailing away, with a sandwich devote.

A crab in shades takes a sunlit stroll,
Shuffling along, like it's got a goal.
With each wave's crash, laughter is found,
As squeals of joy echo all around.

Serenade of the Coral Reefs

The fish wear ties for an ocean ball,
While the sharks are the bouncers, leading it all.
A mermaid with curls makes a big splash,
As she juggles seaweed and a walrus mustache.

An octopus plays a whimsical tune,
Tapping its tentacles to a bright, silver moon.
The clams are the crowd, they cheer and clap,
For every good joke, there's a seaweed rap.

Coral's a canvas for the undersea art,
With starfish dancers, they play every part.
The bubble parade floats by with glee,
In a colorful world, where all are free.

Tides of Time and Memory

The tide rolls in with a playful grin,
As flip-flops dance on the beach again.
A child builds castles of wet, squishy sand,
With a bucket that's won many battles, so grand.

Grandpa's old tales make the crabs roll their eyes,
As he claims he once rode a fish that could fly!
The ocean chuckles at every tall tale,
While the sun flirts freely, leaving a trail.

Waves keep calling, a rhythmic rhyme,
As memories drift like waves over time.
The laughter lingers on salty air,
In a funny dance that we all share.

The Soul of the Emerald Isle

In a land where the grass grows tall,
Leprechauns dance, they heed the call.
With a pint in hand, they jig and sway,
Laughing at clouds that dare to play.

The weather's wild, the skies are bright,
A sunburnt back can spark a fight.
Frogs wear tuxedos, they prance and leap,
While giggling hens plot mischief deep.

The sweet breeze carries laughter far,
As locals shout, "There's a cow in the bar!"
For every joke told, another unfolds,
Around every corner, a new tale holds.

So join the fun, let spirits high,
Dance with the sheep and give it a try.
In this odd land of mirth and cheer,
Where every day's a joke, come here!

Embracing the Warmth of Day

Sipping coconut water on the shore,
Waves crashing gently, what a bore!
Sunblock smeared like war paint bright,
Dodging seagulls that dive for a bite.

Flip-flops flapping on my feet,
A crab scuttles past, oh what a feat!
Sandy towel is now a throne,
As I rule this kingdom all alone.

Palms waving as they tell me tales,
Of tourists lost who followed trails.
With a piña colada by my side,
I've found my place; in sun I abide.

So here's to laughs, let worries fade,
In this sun-drenched life, I'm unafraid.
Give me the beach and a good friend's grin,
Where laughter echoes and fun begins!

Adventures in Tropical Rain

The skies opened wide, a downpour to greet,
I danced along puddles, oh what a treat!
Umbrellas flew by like kites in the air,
As I giggled and slipped without a care.

The frogs serenade with a croak and a cheer,
Each ripple a laugh, each splash brings a tear.
I chased after ducks, they quacked in delight,
In this wacky wet world, I danced through the night.

The colors all pop, so vivid and bright,
Wearing rubber boots, I'm ready for flight.
With rain on my nose, I join the parade,
In this wacky wet wonder, I'll never fade.

So here's to the rain, let umbrellas capsize,
In chaotic delight, we'll wear our surprise.
With each drip, I grin, it's pure, bonkers fun,
In the adventure of droplet and sun!

Sunkissed Reverie

A sun hat so big, it could take flight,
Tripping over flip-flops in pure daylight.
Lemonade spills, a sticky parade,
I laugh at myself, such a mess I've made!

Palm trees shade me from all of my woes,
A crab winks at me, he knows how it goes.
With a wink and a nod, I join in the jest,
In this sudsy sun, I find my rest.

Coconuts roll like balls at the fair,
And sunscreen war paints me here and there.
With friends like these, who needs a plan?
Life's sweetest moments come with a jam!

So raise your drink, let's toast to the sun,
In this quirky place, we're never outdone.
With laughter so loud, we'll dance till the night,
In this sunkissed reverie, everything's right!

Serenade of the Seashells

Oh, the shells sing loud, a joyful tune,
They dance with waves beneath the moon.
A crab with rhythm, a starfish sway,
Inviting all to join the bay.

Seagulls giggle, as they dive and dip,
Clams clap shells in a rhythmic grip.
The ocean's orchestra makes quite a scene,
With sandy solos, if you know what I mean!

Turtles twerk in a beachside show,
While jellyfish jiggle with a luminous glow.
Each tide brings laughter, a light-hearted jest,
In this shellfish concert, you're a welcomed guest!

So come on down, the fun won't cease,
Let the shells serenade and bring you peace.
With each splash and shimmer, mischief runs deep,
In this seaside symphony, you won't lose sleep!

Footprints in Warm Sand

Footprints scatter like whispered tales,
As laughter echoes over sun-kissed trails.
Flip-flops flopping, a tropical sound,
Mischievous sand crabs dance all around.

The waves sneak up, with a playful sneer,
Chasing our toes like it wants us near.
Each print a story, a giggle or two,
The tide rolls in, while the sun says adieu.

Sunburned noses and hats gone astray,
While seagulls plot a sneaky buffet.
The sand gets stuck in the most bizarre places,
As shells give us knowing, silly faces.

Yet we keep running, no moment to waste,
The fun of the shore, too good to be paced.
With footprints behind, we live in delight,
Beneath this great sky, everything feels right!

The Mask of the Rainforest

In the green attire, where the critters play,
A sloth wears sunglasses, saying, 'Hey!'
The monkeys swing in a comical race,
While toucans laugh with a colorful face.

Caterpillars wiggle in a silly parade,
As frogs croak songs in a retro cascade.
With vines that twist like a playful vine,
Join the dance, it's a whimsical time!

Mysterious shadows sneak and then bounce,
While lizards gossip and giggle, espouse.
Rain drizzles down like a cheerful tune,
In the mask of the rainforest, we all are immune!

Wiggy-wag lizards and chatterboxing frogs,
All gather together, ignoring the logs.
Wrapping up fun in each leafy nook,
This rainforest revelry has quite the hook!

Echoes of Laughter in Paradise

In this sunny haven where bright colors bloom,
Laughter echoes, capturing the room.
A parrot squawks out a silly old joke,
As palm trees giggle, swaying their cloak.

Children run wild, with ice cream in hand,
While sun hats fly like they're making a stand.
A playful breeze tosses kites in the air,
With each joyful twirl, we lose all our care.

Surfboards dance on waves, in gleeful ballet,
As dolphins join in, performing on display.
The sun grins wide, like it knows our jest,
In this paradise moment, we truly are blessed!

So come and join, let your troubles go,
In the warm embrace of this laughter flow.
Echoes of joy wrap around so tight,
In this wonderful place, everything's just right!

Shadows of the Island

In the shade, a crab scuttles near,
Waving its claws as if it could cheer.
A parrot squawks, a weird serenade,
While tourists spill drinks—they're quite afraid!

Lizards do yoga, all on a log,
Sunbathing lazy, not caring a smog.
Flip-flops are flying, it's chaos, oh dear!
The chickens just laugh, they have no fear!

Sun-Kissed Shores

With sunscreen slathered, all gleam and glow,
A sunburned fellow screams, "Oh no!"
Beach balls collide with a comical thud,
While kids build sandcastles and laugh in the mud.

Old Uncle Fred jumps in, thinking he's spry,
But misjudges the wave, oh my, oh my!
The umbrella flips over, like a wild kite,
While seagulls dive-bomb, it's quite a sight!

Tales of the Island Dancer

A dancer spins, her grass skirt sways,
Chasing the rhythm through sun-soaked bays.
But watch out for coconuts up in the tree,
They'll land right on you, oh dear, oh me!

The ukulele's strumming, a cheerful sound,
While the dog tries to join, leaping around.
Footloose and fancy, the drinks overflow,
And someone's been caught with a chair in tow!

The Call of the Wild Hibiscus

Hibiscus blooms—what a sight to see,
Dancing in breezes, all wild and free.
But what's that buzzing? A bee in a rush,
It's chasing a flower with quite a fuss!

The hammock's swinging, it's calling my name,
But the cat's claiming it, that's all part of the game.
A mango gets tossed, a hilarious play,
And everyone joins in—what a zany day!

Dreams Under the Mango Tree

A mango drops, splat on my head,
It knocks me out, into dreamland I tread.
I chase after birds with a fruit-filled grin,
And argue with monkeys, oh where do I begin?

The sun's a big orange, rolling on by,
I greet it with laughter, oh my, oh my!
The shade plays tricks, it dances around,
While I'm sprawled in grass, looking foolish and round.

I hear the giggles of distant delight,
As I wrestle the branches, oh what a sight!
The squirrels all snicker, they think I'm a clown,
A king in my kingdom of laughter and brown.

So here I shall stay, in this silliness deep,
Under the mango tree, it's fun times I keep,
For dreams here are sweet, just like the fruit's glow,
And giggles grow louder, the more that I know.

Lanterns of the Evening Sky

The sky's a big canvas, painted with flair,
I toss my old sandals, fly through the air.
With a squeak and a splash, I'm now in a boat,
Giving the waves an impromptu coat.

My friends catch the clouds, they're floating on high,
With laughs and some giggles, we all wave goodbye.
A picnic of stars, we munch in delight,
Oh, what a feast, under this magical night.

The lanterns are blinking, they're winking at me,
They know all my secrets, they're giggling with glee.
I dance with the moon, who's a mischievous pal,
Taking silly photos—each one is a gal.

We twirl with the breezes, we bubble with cheer,
As shadows start telling the stories we hear.
So let's raise a toast, with a cup made of air,
To the laughter and joy, floating up everywhere.

The Aroma of Salt and Spice

The ocean is stinky, but oh so divine,
With fish doing flips like they're one of a kind.
A crab wears a bowtie, struts like a star,
While I'm flipping burgers, you know who you are!

Salted air tickles, oh watch out, it bites,
As I chase flying gulls with my bread, what a sight!
They're swooping and diving, it's pure circus fun,
"Just give back my sandwich!" I shout at the sun.

The spices are dancing, in my pot they spin,
A spoon takes a leap, like it's winning a win!
With chili and garlic, a flavor parade,
I'm laughing so hard, can't believe I'm this made.

So sprinkle some joy, like the salt in the sea,
Let's feast with a gumbo, just you and me,
For the hunger of laughter is best served with spice,
And a side of good humor, which tastes oh so nice!

Starlit Whispers of the Lagoon

The lagoon is a mirror, reflecting my jokes,
As frogs join the chorus, they laugh like old folks.
I slip on a lily and dance a bit wild,
With waves that are giggling, I'm nature's own child.

The fish flip their fins, they're stars in my show,
While turtles bob along, all shouting, "Let's go!"
I splash with the bubbles and dream in my mind,
Of hippos in tutus, they're one of a kind.

The night is a blanket that wraps us in glee,
As the fireflies twinkle like they're teasing me.
The whispers of starlight, they tickle my thoughts,
With jokes from the lagoon, oh, the laughter's red hot!

So let's keep on shining, like lanterns we'll be,
Beneath this great sky, let the fun always free,
For in every splash, every whisper we chase,
Laughter's the treasure, we all know and embrace.

Garden of the Sea

Fish in tuxedos swim by,
Waving their fins, oh so spry.
Coral blooms like a party hat,
Underwater, life's a bit chitchat.

Crabs do the shuffle, not quite a dance,
Seaweed twirls in a flirty chance.
Starfish lounge like they're on a beach,
All calling for a joellyfish each.

Seashells gossip, oh what a sight,
Turtles trade tales, holding them tight.
A dolphin's laugh fills the salty air,
Who knew sea life could be this rare?

With flip-flops on and snorkels too,
The garden of laughs, who knew?
A splash of humor in every wave,
Beneath the surface, fun's all we crave!

The Sound of Serenity

A parrot sings out a quirky tune,
Swinging on branches under the moon.
Monkeys wearing hats check the score,
Playing cards, could there be more?

The river runs deep with a giggly flow,
While frogs hop along, putting on a show.
Crickets drum beats with a flair,
Nature's concert, beyond compare.

A sloth, dressed in slow-motion style,
Slouches in trees, takes a while.
Whispers of wind tickle your ears,
Nature's comedy, wiping your tears.

As the sun dips low, shades of gold,
Each creature's delight starts to unfold.
In the calmest moments, laughs ring clear,
In the sound of laughs, we're ever near!

Kaleidoscope of Jungle Spirits

Lizards wear boots, take the lead,
Strutting their stuff, oh what a breed!
Colors collide in dazzling spree,
Jungle spirits sip tea like it's free.

Butterflies gossip with elegant flair,
Plantain chips scattered without a care.
A jaguar snoozes, dreaming of cake,
In the land of whispers, make no mistake.

Beetles parade in shimmery suits,
Holding a ball, serving up fruits.
The monkeys swing by, cracking a joke,
In this vibrant realm, wake or woke!

Every leaf holds a punchline or two,
In a world where smiles are always due.
Let's join the fun and shout with glee,
In this kaleidoscope, wild and free!

The Lure of the Coral Caves

Mermaids giggle, brushing their hair,
Seahorses prance without a care.
Coral reefs tell tales with flair,
Echoing laughter in salty air.

Octopus painters create with zest,
Twisting colors, they surely are blessed.
With a wink and a nudge, they make their art,
In underwater galleries, it's just the start.

Eels have jokes, they play hide and seek,
Pop out with antics, cheeky, unique.
Fish line up, waiting for the reveal,
In this coral world, all's surreal.

With each splash and each flip and twirl,
The ocean's allure makes the heart whirl.
In this magical cave of delight,
Every wave whispers, come join the night!

Mysteries of the Hidden Lagoon

A catfish wears a tiny hat,
Swimming past a splashing rat.
A turtle plays the secret tune,
While crabs breakdance by the moon.

The otters gossip, splash and dive,
While lily pads form a high five.
A parrot shouts, 'I'm 25!'
As frogs attempt to jog and jive.

Fish hold parties in their schools,
Teaching snails the latest rules.
But in the end, they all agree,
The fish who swims, is never free.

With bubbles popping all around,
The waters dance without a sound.
But here's the best, don't forget:
A gator's tickle is a safe bet!

Symphony of the Teakwood Forest

The trees all sway to tunes unknown,
With squirrels tapping on a phone.
A woodpecker conducts the show,
While rabbits watch the poetry flow.

A raccoon dons a fancy coat,
As fireflies are singing notes.
The bushes hum a lively beat,
While ants serve snacks—what a treat!

In shadows deep, the whispers giggle,
As toads attempt a funny jiggle.
Branches shake and twigs will creak,
In harmony, they all will speak.

So come and dance amidst the trees,
Where nature sways with such great ease.
Join in the fun, let spirits rise,
For in this place, joy never dies!

Sunlit Conversations with the Sea

The waves chat softly, full of cheer,
With jokes that only crabs can hear.
A starfish tells a tale of woe,
As dolphins laugh and steal the show.

Shells gossip about the day's events,
While seagulls claim their share of cents.
A shipwrecked pirate looks so lost,
But finds the ocean, life's sweet cost.

The tide rolls in with funny dreams,
As jellyfish write silly memes.
They float and flop with a burst of glee,
While shrimp compete in a grand spree!

With each splash and glimmering spark,
The sea reveals its playful heart.
So crack a joke, share a grin,
In this watery world, we all win!

Nature's Palette in a Paradise

The daisies wear their brightest hues,
While butterflies sip on morning dew.
A lazy bee hums out a tune,
And ants plan picnics under the moon.

The sunsets paint with brushes wide,
While frogs call out to their bug guide.
Petunias giggle, toss their fluff,
Claiming beauty is never snuff.

A rainbow pops with colors bold,
As leaves play cards, laughing uncontrolled.
While winds carry tales from afar,
Nature's jokes shine like a star.

So gather 'round, for spirits high,
In every bloom, a funny sigh.
Let's laugh at life, let hearts ignite,
In this paradise, pure delight!

Shadows Playing in Sunlit Pools

The lizards dance, with wiggly tails,
While curious crabs wear tiny scales.
A splash and a giggle from the nearby kids,
As they chase a duck on its floating lids.

Sunlight bounces, like a playful cat,
While I ponder on legacies of my old hat.
A cheeky breeze whispers secrets near,
As I search for my lost cool drink in fear.

Palm fronds wave like they're in a race,
And I tripped on a flip-flop, oh what a face!
But laughter erupts when I tumble down,
As shadows chuckle and twirl all around.

So, I lay back, the world a big jest,
In the games of nature, I must invest.
For in this pool where smiles don't fade,
Life's simply a splash of a playful parade.

Vibrant Echoes of Island Life

Fragrant blooms dance with the bees,
Throwing parties on the leaves of trees.
A parrot squawks, wearing a crown,
While I sip coconut, feeling like a clown.

Waves giggle as they tease the shore,
While my sunscreen's stuck, oh such a bore!
The smell of grilled fish fills the air,
As I dodge seagulls, quite the wild affair.

Fishermen swap tales with a wink and grin,
While my fishing line tangles with the bin.
Yet they all laugh when my bait flies free,
Maybe fishing's just not meant for me!

The sunset brings colors that wildly clash,
While I drop my hat in a bright, bold splash.
But island life is always a score,
For laughter and joy are forever in store.

Reflections on a Sapphire Sea

The ocean winks with sparkling glee,
While fish parade like they own the spree.
I squint at the sun, it's lost in my hat,
As I dive for a shell with a big ol' splat!

Jellyfish float by, in capricious moods,
I wave to a dolphin, surrounded by brood.
But my wave was a flop, a splash in the air,
And now I'm drenched, why do I dare?

Mermaids laugh as they comb their hair,
While I chase the crabs without a care.
But one pinches my toe, oh what a scene,
You'd think I'm the star of a silly routine!

Evening rolls in with a blush on its face,
While I trip over sand, in a goofy race.
Yet my heart sings with joy, under skies of blue,
For every moment's a treasure, oh how true!

The Art of Waiting for Sunset

In a hammock swing, I take my seat,
Watching the day with sandals on my feet.
The clock ticks slower than a sleepy snail,
As I plan my dinner, what a grand scale!

Bicycles zoom past with laughter on tow,
While seagulls plot raids on my taco show.
A crow munches crumbs, oh what a thief,
While I stare at the sun with joyful belief.

Hot salsa drips down my chin like rain,
As I contemplate life in this silly game.
But the sun keeps its secrets, never in sight,
As I munch on beach snacks with sheer delight.

Yet when the sky blazes with colors so bold,
I chuckle at time, for stories unfold.
Each sunset a promise, wrapped up tight,
In the laughter of waiting, oh what a delight!

Ripples of Laughter from the Shore

Waves tickle toes, giggles galore,
A crab scuttles sideways, what a chore!
Seagulls squawk gossip, they steal my fries,
In this sandy circus, joy never dies.

Sun hats are flying like kites in the breeze,
Flip-flops are dancing, doing a tease.
The sand's got a secret, it's ticklish, too,
Who knew beaching could give such a view?

Splashing and laughing, let worries float,
A dolphin jumps high, oh what a quote!
Life's like a clam, sometimes it's shy,
But with laughter like bubbles, it'll never die.

So gather round friends, let the stories flow,
With sand in our hair, we steal the show.
Each ripple of laughter, a treasure to keep,
In this shore's grand party, we'll never sleep.

Sun-Kissed Stories of the Isle

A pineapple runs a race, who will win?
The sun sets low, oh let the fun begin!
Lizards in shades, sipping cool lemonade,
With each twist and turn, hilarity's made.

Coconuts roll off, just like our luck,
Who knew beach life could be so stuck?
Sunburned noses tell tales of flair,
As flip-flops fly high through the salty air.

Turtles take bets, who's the quickest of all?
While children build castles, oh they stand tall!
A breeze whispers secrets, it's all in jest,
Under roofs of palm, we find our best.

Wrap me in laughter, let worries dissolve,
The joy on this isle, it's problems we solve.
With each sunlit story, we twirl and spin,
In this paradise dance, everyone's a win!

Dreams Woven in Coconut Leaves

Under the shadows of swaying green,
Coconuts hold secrets, if you know what I mean.
Every leaf's a player in this sunny skit,
As we share dreams that are just a bit lit.

A monkey steals snacks as we laugh and shout,
While the sun throws a party, with warmth all about.
Flip-flops are frolicking, racing the breeze,
In this happy place, oh, just do as you please.

Jellyfish in tutus do the limbo dance,
While the tide takes a photo, it's our last chance.
With coconuts grinning, who needs a show?
Life's a bright party, and we're stealing the glow!

In dreams stitched from laughter, we twirl and weave,
With joy as our fabric, there's nothing we grieve.
So join in the chorus, let the laughter fly,
With coconut dreams, we can surely touch the sky.

Traces of Footprints in the Soft Sand

Footprints weave stories, a playful parade,
As the sun writes designs in the sandy braid.
A dog steals my snack, what a sneaky pup,
Who knew this coastline could shake you up?

The water winks back, it's a cheeky tease,
While seaweed plays dress-up in the warm breeze.
Each step is a giggle, on this playful floor,
We jump and we twirl, forever wanting more.

With laughter as catchy as waves on the shore,
Each splish-splash adventure opens a door.
The tide rushes in, stealing all our tracks,
But with hugs and high-fives, we don't hold back.

So leave your footprints, let them drift away,
In this sandy wonderland, we dance and sway.
With every wave's whisper, our laughter remains,
In this sunny paradise, we're breaking chains.

Blossoms Amidst Silence

In the garden, bugs do tango,
Flowers wear their socks all wringed.
Bees take turns, a buzz like banjo,
While the petals laugh and sing.

A snail speeds past, I'm quite impressed,
He's off to catch a show at eight.
But I'm stuck here, feeling stressed,
His pace? I can only imitate.

The sun is hot, my drink's a drip,
I shake my head, we're out of ice.
A lizard slips and takes a trip,
Rides the fountain, oh, how nice!

Amidst the blooms, the wise arise,
Gossip flows like breezy frays.
In this silence, laughter lies,
Turns the day to one big play.

Winds of Change in Paradise

A coconut fell—who's to blame?
It bonked a parrot on the head.
He squawks and flutters, what a shame,
Now he's doing a dance instead.

The hammock sways, what a bright sight,
We're flying off to Mars today!
But with my luck, I'll lose my bite,
As space is lacking chips, they say.

Palm trees laugh, they joke around,
With every gust, they flip and twist.
The crabs just roll, they think profound,
"Life's better sideways, don't resist!"

So here's to breezes, laughter free,
The winds of change so wildly spun.
I sip my drink, not caring, see?
Adventure started; let's have fun!

The Allure of the Riviera Sun

The chairs are stacked; it's a true test,
To find the best spot for my tan.
A gull swoops down, now that's a jest,
Stealing fries with a master plan.

The waves crash in with salty cheer,
Each splash a joke upon the shore.
I duck and dodge, oh dear, oh dear,
But splashes can't ruin my rapport.

My flip-flops sing a tuneful song,
While sunscreen lingers—what a blob!
With every step, I dance along,
Like I'm the star in this sunbob.

When twilight comes, the stars align,
The evening calls for coconut fun.
I raise my glass, and all is fine,
Under the charm of the warm sun.

Tales Told by the Bay

Fish gather 'round, it's story night,
With tales of hooks that got away.
They laugh and giggle—a splendid sight,
As I munch popcorn, in dismay.

The crab recounts his dance with fate,
"Caught in a bucket, felt so strange."
"We feasted on fries, oh, wasn't it great?
But never again, I'll make a change!"

The moon's eavesdropping on each word,
Mimicking laughs, the tide rolls high.
Each story loops—a tangled herd,
From shrimp to eel, they wink and sigh.

So gather 'round, you merry crowd,
The bay's full of secrets and glee.
With chuckles loud, they're truly proud,
These fishy tales are wild and free.

Laughter at High Tide

The crabs dance sideways on the sand,
While seagulls squawk the band's demand.
Children splash and giggle with glee,
As waves tickle toes, and that's the key.

Sun hats flying, laughter blends,
Ice cream faces, sticky friends.
A flip-flop flings, it's quite a sight,
As beach balls soar in sheer delight.

Sandy sandwiches get a bit chewed,
While sunscreen fights the sun's rude mood.
Flip, flop, splash, it's all in fun,
Who knew the beach could weigh a ton?

As sunset paints the ocean bright,
We laugh at shadows, what a sight!
Tomorrow's plans, we'll surely break,
But now let's just eat this cheese cake.

Visions of a Sun-Drenched Oasis

A hammock swings, but not for long,
As squirrels drop nuts — it seems so wrong!
Ice drinks spill from hands that slip,
While kids go swimming — oh, wait, a trip!

Coconuts roll in a dance of fate,
One lands on a hat; oh, how great!
The parrot squawks a tune so fine,
But really just wants a sip of wine.

Mosquitoes take to the air with flair,
While we swat and scream, lose all our hair.
Meanwhile, a toddler shows off their sway,
In a dance-off that makes my day!

Under palm trees, we break into song,
It's a paradise where we won't stay long.
But for now, some laughter and sun,
In the land where shenanigans run.

The Kiss of the Ocean Mist

A splash of waves, a gasp of air,
The dog steals snacks without a care.
The misty breeze, a gentle tease,
As everyone's hair resembles the trees.

In flip-flops fighting against the tide,
Some brave souls decide to go for a ride.
The beach ball flies, the giggles soar,
But who kicked it into the old man's drawer?

A sunburned nose, truly a sight,
As jokes fly fast into the night.
The ocean pulls in its playful grip,
While seagulls scold from their cornered trip.

As the sun dips low, we make a pact,
To bring next time our laughter intact.
With memories made, like sand in our toes,
We'll cherish this moment, as friendship grows.

Tranquility Under the Palms

Palms sway gently with a rhythmic charm,
While tourists trip, it's hard to keep calm.
Sipping coconut, oh what a delight,
But there goes my straw, oh what a fright!

Turtles plod slowly, no rush at all,
While kids chase waves that seem so small.
Beach bells jingle, a catchy refrain,
As my hat lands on a passing train!

The sun loves to play hide and seek,
While picnic ants have a feast this week.
"The more, the merrier," as they always say,
But I didn't mean lunch for bugs today!

As daylight fades, we gather silly tales,
Of sunburns, spills, and stolen sails.
Laughter rings loud amidst palmy shade,
A whimsical dance we've all made.

Heartbeats in the Tropics

The parrot squawks a tune, oh dear,
While sipping on his cold, cold beer.
The monkeys laugh, they swing and play,
They dance like no one's watching today.

The sunbeam's got a golden grin,
As lizards join the cha-cha spin.
A crab in shorts says, "Hey, let's snack!"
While beach balls bounce, no time to slack.

While tourists tan with heads so red,
A man falls face-first, he's lost his tread.
The waves come in and pull us back,
"Oh look, another soda attack!"

The rhythm of this island life,
Is full of giggles, minus strife.
With every heartbeat, fun's a must,
In this land of laughter and of rust.

Swaying Silhouettes at Dusk

Dancing shadows on the sand,
A coconut slips from my hand.
The palm trees sway, they think it's grand,
While I trip over my own band.

A sunset cocktail, bright and bold,
But now my drink's got turned to gold.
The fish jump up for one last splash,
And now I'm feeling quite the gash.

Fishermen in boats look so fine,
As they argue who caught the big fish line.
"It's just a tuna!" one guy yells,
While the sea laughs at their petty swells.

As the darkness starts to grow,
The stars appear in a dazzling show.
With laughter echoing through the night,
This goofy scene feels just right.

A Canvas of Tropical Blooms

The flowers painted, colors bright,
One pink petal takes off in flight.
A bee buzzes with a cheeky grin,
While ants argue about who's in.

With petals soft like fluffy clouds,
The gardener sings, just a bit loud.
A sunflower winks, not very shy,
As butterflies dance and wonder why.

A cactus wears a funny hat,
Says, "Why not?" to a sleepy cat.
And all around this floral cheer,
Are curious bugs, they volunteer.

Nature's canvas, wild and free,
A sweet bouquet of jubilee.
With every bloom, a chuckle's found,
In this garden where joy's unbound.

Moonlit Reflections on the Waves

The moon rolls out, all big and bright,
A fish jumps up, it's quite the sight!
The waves keep talking, bubbly and loud,
As I drift by, feeling quite proud.

A starfish shimmies, striking a pose,
While sea turtles nap, dreaming of prose.
The jellyfish put on a light show,
"Come join the fun!" they say, "Oh don't be slow!"

With every splash, a giggle grows,
As pirates waltz with funny bows.
More antics rise with ocean's swell,
It's a nightly show, under their spell.

So laugh in the glow of this silly scene,
With sea critters' antics, it's all routine.
The ocean sings in soft refrains,
Where joy just dances, and nothing wanes.

Starry Nights Over Gentle Waters

The moon's a big cheese in the sky,
Fish are dancing, oh so spry!
Crabs join in with a clattering sound,
As the mermaids are twirling around.

Stars are gossiping, sharing their tales,
While the turtles are playing with their sails.
A dolphin lets out a giggly bark,
While the night sneaks in, oh so stark.

Jellyfish shyly wave their lights,
And glow like disco balls in the nights.
Seagulls snicker as they fly by,
It's a laughter party under the sky.

Laughter rings out over gentle dips,
As sea urchins throw their weekend trips.
The ocean's a comedy, rolling in waves,
All the fishy folks are the jolly knaves.

Play of Light on Waves

Sunbeams prance like they're on a spree,
While sea turtles sip their fruity tea.
Waves clap hands as they roll ashore,
"Let's surf the coconut wave!" they roar.

Crabs juggle shells with a cheerful grin,
Pretending to be the island's kin.
Seashells giggle under sunny rays,
Whispering secrets in playful ways.

The sun tickles the ocean's face,
While fish are putting on a race.
"Watch me splash!" calls a cheeky trout,
While the waves cheer, laughing out loud.

Seagulls take selfies, striking a pose,
Coconut drinks are the fashion, I suppose.
The sea dances intensely, it's quite a sight,
All in good humor, from morning till night.

The Rhythm of the Trade Winds

Breezes sneak in like giggly thieves,
Stealing hats from palm tree leaves.
Kites flutter about, soaring high,
While the islanders simply sigh.

A monkey swings with flair and style,
With a cheeky grin that won't reconcile.
The winds are whispering silly jokes,
As sea cucumbers shake and poke.

Fruits roll down in a playful chase,
While sandcastles hold a race.
Crabs wear sunglasses and strut their stuff,
"Oh, this island life is quite enough!"

Amidst the sway, laughter takes flight,
As shadows stretch into the night.
Trade winds carry tales all around,
Tickling the imagination, so profound.

In the Embrace of Lush Canopies

Leaves are laughing, swinging from trees,
As monkeys munch their bananas with ease.
The toucans gossip over juicy fruit,
While insects dance in their tiny suit.

The breeze rustles, a faux pas here,
A lizard slips, but shows no fear.
Squirrels play hide-and-seek with a grin,
As a butterfly flies lazily in.

Vines tangle like jokes from a friend,
As the blossoms bloom, around the bend.
The jungle's a party, oh what a sight!
With critters who laugh from morning to night.

Under the canopy, the fun's never done,
As nature rejoices, life's great hum.
With each rustle, a giggle escapes,
Turning the ordinary into grand shapes.

Serengeti of Solar Gold

In golden grass, the lions laugh,
A herd of wildebeests takes a gaffe.
Zebras wear stripes, oh what a sight,
Playing hopscotch with the lion's bite.

Elephants march, holding their nose,
Waving at tourists, striking a pose.
Giraffes peep over the tall bushes,
Bumping heads for some silly crushes.

The sun shines bright, makes every hair frizz,
As monkeys chatter, 'What's all this fizz?'
A parrot yells, "I'm the feathered boss!"
While one cheeky squirrel just shouts, "Let's floss!"

In this golden land, so full of cheer,
Even the rhinos shed a tear.
Laughter echoes through the savanna wide,
As nature plays and takes us for a ride.

Tangles of Joy in the Tropics

Coconuts roll and monkeys swing,
In the heart of the jungle, you can hear them sing.
Parrots are gossiping in a colorful spree,
While iguanas lounge, sipping iced sweet tea.

Lizards are dancing on a sunny log,
Each step a wonder, each move a fog.
The crab in the sand wears a tiny crown,
Boasting about his life in a beachside town.

A pineapple slips, goes down with a splash,
A tourist trips over a sea turtle's sash.
Sunburnt and laughing, they both scream,
"I came for the waves but got caught in a dream!"

The breeze brings whispers, so sweet and sly,
Telling secrets of how time can fly.
In tangled vines, the fun never stops,
It's a wildlife party and nobody flops!

Whispers of a Sunlit Shore

On sandy dunes where seagulls flirt,
Children build castles, not quite expert.
Each wave that crashes brings giggles galore,
As shells and treasures roll on the floor.

The sun blares down, a golden mini-drum,
While crab soccer teams go 'whack' with a thrum.
Picnics of laughter, with sandwiches wide,
As jellyfish float with nothing to hide.

Flip-flops flying with every wild kick,
Catching some air, it's the beach day trick.
A wave takes a sip from the lost picnic,
"Oh, there went my lunch!"—it's truly comic!

But every mishap brings shared delight,
As groups of sun-kissed friends unite.
Stories unravel under the warm beams,
In whispers of joy, where laughter redeems.

Dance of the Island Breeze

A hula dancer sways, she's got the flair,
While goofy tourists don grass hats with care.
They shuffle their feet, whose step's offbeat?
To the rhythm of the waves, they admit defeat.

The sun melts gold on the ocean's skin,
As dolphins play hopscotch, with a cheeky grin.
Each flip a splash, oh, what a display,
While the surfboards grind in a sunny ballet.

Palm trees sway in a gusty embrace,
Doing the twist in a leafy race.
A crab in a tuxedo, he's ready to prance,
Challenging all for a grand crabs' dance!

With laughter that tickles the sun-soaked air,
The island breeze laughs without a care.
In this joyful jig where smiles cascade,
Every moment feels like a fun masquerade.

Delights of the Morning Mist

The roosters crow with all their might,
As fog creeps in, a ghostly sight.
Coconut trees sway, lose their stance,
While locals trip in a sleepy dance.

Waves crash softly, the surf's a tease,
A pair of flip-flops loses its ease.
Mornings here bring giggles and grins,
As even the parrots do silly spins.

Coffee brews with a cheerful cheer,
But wait! What's that? Is it a deer?
Nope, just a goat dressed up in style,
Making us laugh when we see it smile.

But as the mist begins to fade,
And sunlight shines on the beach parade.
We chase the shadows, we chase the grin,
In morning's magic, let the fun begin!

The Heartbeat of the Island

A ukulele strums, fills the air,
As tourists twirl in a frantic scare.
Hula dancers wiggle, can't find their place,
While locals laugh—what a funny race!

Banana peels, oh what a slip,
As someone tries to take a dip.
An octopus sneaks in for a swim,
But it's a crab that's caught on film.

The sun will set, but laughter stays,
As folks recount their silly ways.
Silly hats and mismatched shoes,
It's a fashion show they can't refuse.

So dance to the beat, let worries fly,
Grab a pineapple slice, give it a try.
With giggles, grins, and good heartbeats,
This island life is full of treats!

Legends of the Coconut Grove

In the grove, the coconuts fall,
Some mistaken for a bouncy ball.
A penguin struts with a wobbly flair,
As everyone stops to stare and stare.

Whispers of legends fill the dreamy night,
Of mermaids who dabble in playful flight.
But then you'll see, it's a playful shark,
With rubber ducky sailing in the dark.

Tropical drinks spill over the bar,
With umbrellas swaying, oh what a star!
The bartender juggles, what a wild show,
While everyone cheers for the coconut blow.

So come join the fun, don't just observe,
In this grove, it's a twist and curve.
Where laughter's a legend, joy implements,
In the tales we weave, our humor's immense!

Savory Flavors of the Ocean

A fish swims by with an enticing grin,
But wait, that's my dinner wearing a fin!
The chef throws spices like confetti bright,
While seagulls squawk their culinary plight.

Tacos dance on the plate with glee,
As coral reefs join in jovially.
The crabs do the cha-cha on the shore,
A feast of flavors you can't ignore.

Shrimp cocktails curtsy, the calamares twirl,
While seaweed noodles make you want to swirl.
Lobsters pinch at the bubbly tide,
As people laugh, this taste they can't hide.

So grab a fork, don't hesitate!
In this seafood jamboree, it's never late.
For every bite is a giggling delight,
And flavors that dance from morning to night!

Murmurs of the Underbrush

Cockroaches conspire, with crumbs as their prize,
Whispers of mischief, beneath leafy skies.
Lizards in tuxedos, slick and so sly,
Debating their options, like suave little guys.

Frogs hold a concert, croaking with glee,
A symphony of chaos, for all creatures to see.
Crickets are judges, with rules quite absurd,
Laughter erupts at the silliest word.

Ants choreograph dances, in perfect parade,
With tiny tuxedos, they cartwheel and fade.
They march with precision, never a fumble,
While nearby a snail just takes time to stumble.

Beneath woven branches, the laughter abounds,
Where folly is currency, and joy knows no bounds.
Every creature is buzzing, in this vibrant bazaar,
Life's rich tapestry woven like an old guitar.

Paradise Found in Golden Rays

Silly birds chatter, gossip in trees,
Fashion advice from the buzzing honeybees.
Monkeys play tag; they swing with pure flair,
Falling off branches without any care.

A turtle in shades, sunbathing with pride,
Who knew it would take so long for a ride?
In puddles they splash, a hilarious scene,
Jumping like kangaroos, far too keen.

Coconuts tumble, an unplanned surprise,
Splatting on heads, oh what a disguise!
With giggles and chuckles, the chaos unfolds,
In a land where the laughter is more than gold.

When the sun peaks high, and the humor ignites,
Every creature joins in, sharing delight.
In this paradise, with laughter to share,
Life's a quirky dance, in the warm summer air.

Horizon's Embrace at Twilight

As daylight falters, mischief begins,
Squirrels in jammies plotting their spins.
The sunset's a painter, with colors so bold,
While crickets recite tales that never get old.

A raccoon with a mask, planning a heist,
Searching the picnic where snacks are enticed.
Fireflies twinkle, like stars having fun,
Dancing in circles, 'til the day is done.

Beneath the cool shadows, laughter ignites,
With jesters of nature, performing at nights.
An owl gives a wink, as if to say,
Life's a grand joke, it's just the right way.

As stars start to twinkle, the laughter remains,
In this whimsical world, joy freely reigns.
Where every small creature, from dusk until dawn,
Finds humor and fun, until the first yawn.

The Dance of Butterflies

Fluttering wonders in extravagant flair,
Twisting and swirling, without any care.
Chasing the breezes, they tease and they glide,
Carrying giggles, on wings far and wide.

One landed on a nose, oh what a sight!
Creating a ruckus, such delicate flight.
With colors ablaze, they giggle and zoom,
Drawing in laughter, like a sweet blooming bloom.

A snail joins the party, so sluggish, so slow,
But dances with flair; putting on quite the show.
Round and round they twirl, a delightful parade,
As chubby, bouncy beetles applaud, unafraid.

In rhythms of nature, they laugh and they play,
Under bright skies, as they frolic all day.
The world's their stage, beneath warmth's warm kiss,
Every moment a giggle, it simply can't miss.

Memories in a Hammock

Swinging gently, I take a nap,
Dreaming of flying with my cat.
Fried plantains make me giggle loud,
As I snore beneath the leafy shroud.

Friends bring coconuts, a giant feast,
We giggle, gossip, never cease.
A squirrel steals my flip-flop shoe,
And now my pantless days ensue!

Laughter echoes, filling the air,
Sunshine dances in my messy hair.
Trips to the market become a game,
Where rhymes and riddles earn us fame.

Every sip of juice feels like a cheer,
To celebrate life, year after year.
We float on waves, no worries come,
Sipping sweet sunshine, feeling so dumb.

Beyond the Horizon's Glow

A parrot squawks, such a noisy fellow,
As I try to dance all sweet and mellow.
Crabs in the sand, doing the cha-cha,
I trip and tumble like a klutzy star!

Seagulls laugh like they own the sky,
While I juggle mangoes, oh my, oh my!
The ocean winks, with bubbles that pop,
Sometimes I wonder, will this ever stop?

A beach ball bounces, hitting my head,
As I tumble back onto the sandbed.
We gather around for a sandcastle race,
Every victory feels like a big embrace.

So we sip cold drinks, the party's on,
Chasing each other till the twilight's gone.
With sunset smiles and tanned-up skin,
We'll keep these memories where laughter's been.

The Color of Tides

The ocean is blue, but my toes are green,
From all the algae I've grazed, it seems.
Shells in my bucket, treasures galore,
All the weird finds, who could ask for more?

Pink flamingos dance by the driftwood,
I'm convinced they think they're really good.
They strut and laugh, heads held so high,
While I chase after them, oh my, oh my!

Seashells play music beneath my feet,
With rhythms that make my dancing sweet.
A wave crashes, I splash like a fish,
It's a silly moment, oh what a wish!

As the sun dips low, the colors ignite,
A canvas of giggles, pure delight.
Every wave whispers a joke or two,
I'll laugh till I cry, just me and the blue.

Journey to the Heart of Paradise

On a boat made of laughter, we sail away,
With pirate hats that make the seagulls sway.
An octopus juggling, such a sight to see,
I'll trade him my sandwich, just not my tea!

Lost in the jungle, oh where's my shoe?
The monkeys are laughing, oh what to do?
A toucan bellows a pun so bad,
We all burst out, it's the best we've had!

Mangoes drop like gifts from the trees,
We catch them with giggles, shared with ease.
Frogs play hopscotch on lily pads bright,
Every leap, hysterical, in golden light.

As we reach the heart, the stars start to twinkle,
Our adventure, a puzzle, full of a sprinkle.
With belly laughs and a sprinkle of fun,
This journey, my friends, has just begun!

Whispers of the Coastal Breeze

The seagull squawked, a silly tune,
While sunbathers juggled coconut spoons.
Sandcastles crumbled with a puff of air,
As kids chased their dreams, without a care.

The surfboards twirled, a wobbly dance,
Caught in the waves, not a single chance.
Laughter erupted as we took a spill,
Splashing around, it's such a thrill!

Umbrellas flipped, a wild parade,
As sunscreen got squirted, a slippery cascade.
With sunhats askew, we danced on the shore,
Our goofy moves beckon laughter galore.

Each wave brings a giggle, a trip and a fall,
Beach games a-jiving, come one, come all!
The adventure continues, not a dull day,
As fun is the rule in this seaside play.

Dance of the Palms at Dusk

The palms sway gently, a comical sight,
Like dancers in training, too tipsy to write.
A crab crabs its way in a hurry to glide,
As tourists all gather, no need to hide.

A hammock swings low, a nap turned to snooze,
While a cheeky monkey steals someone's shoes.
We toast to the sunset, with drinks in hand,
Mixing laughter and fun, just as we planned.

Fireflies twinkle with little bright sparks,
As the night sings to us with its quirky remarks.
The breeze carries jokes that make us all grin,
As the stars join the party, let the fun begin!

A conch shell sounds, signaling cheer,
With every absurd moment, we hold dear.
The world is our stage, let's dance till we drop,
In the glow of dusk, we're never gonna stop!

Secrets of the Lush Green Canopy

In the dappled shade, a parrot does squawk,
While monkeys play tag, mocking our walk.
Vines swinging lower, just dodging our heads,
Nature's own theater, silliness spreads.

Under the leaves, we tell silly tales,
Of pirates and treasures and oversized gales.
A toucan with style is a sight to behold,
Stealing the show, with feathers of gold.

A tree frog croaks, in its best opera voice,
Causing even the insects to giggle by choice.
The rustle of branches brings a comic tune,
As we dance through the green, 'neath the mischievous moon.

Adventure awaits in this leafy domain,
As smiles and fun keep growing like grain.
With every green secret, our laughter does thrive,
In this quirky jungle, we come alive!

Radiance of the Island Sky

Clouds float like marshmallows, fluffy and bright,
While sunbeams play tag as they peek into sight.
A pelican's dive brings splashes and cheers,
As children rejoice, spilling juice on their peers.

Flip-flops are flying, a fashion faux pas,
As someone slips over a coconut jar.
With hats turned askew and sunglasses askew,
We're the kings of the beach, at least, that's our view!

Sipping on smoothies, flavors galore,
Mixing banana with a bit of uproar.
The sunset paints laughter with colors so bright,
As we dance in the glow, a truly wild sight.

Finally, as day takes its sweet bow,
With memories crafted, we take a deep vow,
To cherish this laughter shared under the sky,
For life's the best comedy — oh me, oh my!

The Solstice of Brightness and Shade

Palm trees dance with the breeze,
Shadows loom like friendly tease.
Sunglasses perched upon my nose,
I trip and fall—how nature knows!

Coconuts drop from lofty heights,
I duck and dodge, oh what a plight!
Laughter spills like tropical rain,
As crabs join in, they know my pain.

Flip-flops flapping, taking flight,
Where did they go? Out of my sight!
Sunburns forming in awkward spots,
Ice cream melting—those tasty thoughts!

In this land of fun and cheer,
Every mishap ends in a sneer.
So here's to laughter under rays,
Life's a joke in sunny days!

Threads of Light Through Palm Fronds

Sunbeams slide through leafy screens,
Tickling toes in vibrant sheens.
Lizards watch with knowing grins,
As I attempt to dance, it spins!

Fronds above provide a show,
As I chase shadows to and fro.
A breeze brings scents of coconut,
But my feet trip—now that is nuts!

Sunscreen's slathered on in haste,
But I smell more like a taste!
The local birds chuckle and squawk,
My running turns to silly walk.

In threads of sunlight life unwinds,
With jokes and jests, pure joy it finds.
So grab a drink, let laughter flow,
Under the palms where antics grow!

Melodies from the Hibiscus Blooms

Hibiscus bloom, their colors bright,
Swaying gently in the light.
Butterflies flirt and take a spin,
While I try to join, but just grin.

Bees hum songs of sweet delight,
While I dance with all my might.
Falling petals, a vibrant rain,
I trip, but laugh through all the pain!

Laughter echoes, birds take wing,
As I bungle this funny fling.
Nature chuckles at my fumble,
The hibiscus blooms just tumble.

In this garden, joy abounds,
With silly steps and silly sounds.
Let's twirl around, embrace the cheer,
As every bloom hums laughter here!

www.ingramcontent.com/pod-product-compliance
Lightning Source LLC
Chambersburg PA
CBHW052221090526
44585CB00015BA/1406